QUOTABLE QUOTES

QUOTABLE QUOTES

WIT & WISDOM FROM 100 YEARS OF READER'S DIGEST

Reader's Digest

NEW YORK/MONTREAL

INTRODUCTION

From the very first issue of *Reader's Digest* published in February 1922, pithy sayings from the great minds of the day were an integral part of the magazine–the ultimate *Reader's Digest* version of wit and wisdom, as it were. Quotable Quotes, as it appears today, first ran in the January 1934 issue. Much as it does today, the column included advice and observations on a broad array of topics from both living and deceased people from all walks of life. The carefully curated collection here will motivate, inspire, entertain, and delight, as Quotable Quotes always has.

❖ ❖ ❖

from Remarkable Remarks, February 1922

Women love men for wanting to be mothered.
–ETHEL BARRYMORE

Boys nowadays take advice and then do as they please.
–JOHN D. ROCKEFELLER

The biggest liar in the world is They Say.
–DOUGLAS MALLOCH

Kindness consists in loving people more than they deserve.

–JOSEPH JOUBERT

The most beautiful
thing in the world is, of
course, the world itself.

–WALLACE STEVENS

✦ ✦ ✦

Swift gratitude
is the sweetest.

–GREEK PROVERB

I challenge anybody in their darkest moment to write what they're grateful for, even stupid little things like green grass or a friendly conversation with somebody on the elevator. You start to realize how rich you are.

—*JIM CARREY*

Resolve to be tender with the young, compassionate with the aged, sympathetic with the striving, and tolerant with the weak and the wrong. Sometime in life you will have been all of these.

—BOB GODDARD

It's a lot more satisfying
to reach for the stars
even if you only end up
landing on the moon.

–KERMIT THE FROG

He turns not back who is bound to a star.

–LEONARDO DA VINCI

The man who forgets
to be grateful has
fallen asleep in life.

–ROBERT LOUIS STEVENSON

There is perhaps no one of our natural passions so hard to subdue as pride. Beat it down, stifle it, mortify it as much as one pleases, it is still alive. Even if I could conceive that I had completely overcome it, I should probably be proud of my humility.

—BENJAMIN FRANKLIN

We cherish our friends
not for their ability
to amuse us, but for our
ability to amuse them.

–EVELYN WAUGH

We either make
ourselves miserable
or strong. The amount
of work is the same.

–CARLOS CASTENEDA

✦ ✦ ✦

Wisdom outweighs
any wealth.

–SOPHOCLES

We are happy when we have family, we are happy when we have friends, and almost all the other things we think make us happy actually are just ways of getting more family and friends.

—*DANIEL GILBERT*

Both men and women should feel free to be sensitive. Both men and women should feel free to be strong ... It is time that we all perceive gender on a spectrum, not as two opposing sets of ideals.

—*EMMA WATSON*

I have never considered compassion a finite resource.

–ROXANE GAY

Wit has truth in it;
wisecracking is simply
calisthenics with words.

–DOROTHY PARKER

♦ ♦ ♦

A good laugh and a long
sleep are the best cures
in the doctor's book.

–IRISH PROVERB

Sometimes you are born into a family. Sometimes you need to go find it. Sometimes it finds you. But no matter how it comes together, when it does, family is what you fight for.

—SANDRA BULLOCK

Eventually, I began to understand my mother's mantra that "the time of day belongs to everyone." After years of walking into grocery stores, the post office, and meeting friends and strangers along the way, I finally understood her homespun expression: She meant everyone deserves a kind word.

—AL ROKER

We're all so busy chasing the extraordinary that we forget to stop and be grateful for the ordinary.

–BRENÉ BROWN

SUCCESS

A surplus of effort could overcome
a deficit of confidence.

—SONIA SOTOMAYOR

◆

Start unknown, finish unforgettable.

—MISTY COPELAND

◆

If my mind can conceive it,
and my heart can believe it,
I know I can achieve it.

—*THE REV. JESSE JACKSON*

If you're willing to fail interestingly, you tend to succeed interestingly.

—*EDWARD ALBEE*

✦

It is not the mountain that we conquer, but ourselves.

—*SIR EDMUND HILLARY*

✦

Sometimes it's the people you can't help who inspire you the most.

—*MELINDA GATES*

The world does not deliver meaning to you. You have to make it meaningful ... and decide what you want and need and must do.

—*ZADIE SMITH*

If you want to walk fast,
walk alone; if you want to
walk far, walk with others.

–AFRICAN PROVERB

✦ ✦ ✦

All our dreams can
come true if we have the
courage to pursue them.

–WALT DISNEY

If a man happens to
find himself, he has a
mansion which he can
inhabit with dignity
all the days of his life.

–JAMES A. MICHENER

Teach, volunteer, show up at PTA meetings, show up at the Boys & Girls Club, vote, march, be a citizen. Because in a world of bullets and bots, divisions and distractions, we need more citizens pulling us together instead of trying to pull us apart. Give back to your home as the kind of citizen who builds bridges. Home shapes you. You make sure you shape it back.

—QUEEN LATIFAH

If you've lived well, your smile lines are in the right places.

–JENNIFER GARNER

I could give example after example of how doing the right thing ended up making us more money.

–YVON CHOUINARD

Who wants to reach the end of their life in a perfectly preserved body? The scars and the crinkles and the cracks are what make us interesting.

—*BEAR GRYLLS*

Sometimes you lie in
bed at night and don't
have a single thing
to worry about.
That always worries me.

–CHARLIE BROWN

If you give everybody a
slice of pie, you will still
have more than enough.

–JAY LENO

✦ ✦ ✦

I have witnessed the
softening of the hardest of
hearts by a simple smile.

–GOLDIE HAWN

I've loved quite a few people, and by that I mean I really feel happy in their company. That's pretty much it—the joy of someone's company. That's what I call love.

—*JONI MITCHELL*

True heroism ... is not the urge to surpass all others at whatever cost but the urge to serve others at whatever cost.

—*ARTHUR ASHE*

Everybody is ignorant, only on different subjects.

–WILL ROGERS

We are not held back
by the love we didn't
receive in the past, but
by the love we're not
extending in the present.

–MARIANNE WILLIAMSON

It's so easy to be negative in this world and to say no. Yes is so much better. You say yes when you have your first kiss, when you want to make someone feel good, when you open yourself to new experiences. I always say yes–sì, sì, sì!–and it makes every day better.

—ANDREA BOCELLI

It's the great gift of human beings that we have this power of empathy ... We can all sense a mysterious connection to each other.

—*MERYL STREEP*

I always say, "Don't make plans, make options."

✦ ✦ ✦

If we live good lives, the times are also good. As we are, such are the times.

—ST. AUGUSTINE

You can't connect the dots looking forward; you can only connect them looking backward. So you have to trust that the dots will somehow connect ... You have to trust in something–your gut, destiny, life, karma.

—*STEVE JOBS*

Nobody looks crazy when they're having fun.

–AMY POEHLER

A cynic is a man who knows
the price of everything
and the value of nothing.

–OSCAR WILDE

✦ ✦ ✦

Keep some room in your
heart for the unimaginable.

–MARY OLIVER

I haven't the slightest idea how to change people, but still I keep a long list ... just in case I should ever figure it out.

—*DAVID SEDARIS*

Idleness is not just a vacation, an indulgence, or a vice. The space and quiet [it] provides is a necessary condition for standing back from life and seeing it whole. It is, paradoxically, necessary to getting work done.

—*TIM KREIDER*

Don't say yes to
everything. "No" is also
an answer, and it can
be a full sentence.

–CYNTHIA ERIVO

Success covers a multitude of blunders.

–GEORGE BERNARD SHAW

At close to 99, I can tell you I've never lived alone. I've never laughed alone. And that has as much to do with my being here today as anything else.

–NORMAN LEAR

The really important kind of freedom involves attention and awareness and discipline, and being able truly to care about other people and to sacrifice for them over and over in myriad petty, unsexy ways every day.

—*DAVID FOSTER WALLACE*

Everybody thinks of
changing humanity
and nobody thinks of
changing himself.

–LEO TOLSTOY

"Life is short" really means
"Do something."

–*CHIMAMANDA NGOZI ADICHIE*

✦ ✦ ✦

There's nothing you've ever
been successful at that you
didn't work on every day.

–*WILL SMITH*

People always say to me, "Why are you in such good shape?" and I always answer, "If I told you that you were going to be on film on a 40-foot screen with your shirt off, you'd be in good shape too."

—*HUGH JACKMAN*

Prayer is when you talk to God.
Meditation is when you're listening.
Playing the piano allows you to
do both at the same time.

—*KELSEY GRAMMER*

Failure is the condiment that gives success its flavor.

—TRUMAN CAPOTE

Until I feared I would lose it,
I never loved to read.
One does not love breathing.

–HARPER LEE

✦ ✦ ✦

I have decided to stick
to love ... hate is too great
a burden to bear.

–MARTIN LUTHER KING JR.

I've always been motivated more by negative comments than by positive ones. I know what I do well. Tell me what I don't do well.

—*ABBY WAMBACH*

I realized that part of my identity is saying no to things I don't wanna do ... It is your right to choose what you do and don't do. It is your right to choose what you believe in and don't believe in. It is your right to curate your life and your own perspective.

—*LADY GAGA*

The most common way
people give up their
power is by thinking they
don't have any.

–ALICE WALKER

FAMILY

You don't choose your family.
They are God's gift to you, as you are to them.
—DESMOND TUTU

✦

A couple that golfs together stays together.
Where else can I walk six miles and talk to my
husband for four hours without distraction?
—NORAH O'DONNELL

✦

Every child begins the world again.
—HENRY DAVID THOREAU

We can't give our children the future,
strive though we may to make it secure.
But we can give them the present.

—KATHLEEN NORRIS

✦

There is no such thing as fun for the whole family.

—JERRY SEINFELD

✦

There's nothing better than being home on
a Friday night and eating pizza ... I'm a mom
and a wife and that's what I like to be.

—REESE WITHERSPOON

Life isn't based on the tennis game I play. It's little things. Saying hello to everyone you meet. That's more validating than whether I win a match.

—*NAOMI OSAKA*

As I like to say, take
the shot, even if your
knees are shaking.

–ROBIN ROBERTS

◆ ◆ ◆

A man who builds his
own pedestal had better
use strong cement.

–ANNA QUINDLEN

A leader takes people
where they want to go.
A great leader takes
people where they don't
necessarily want to go,
but ought to be.

–ROSALYNN CARTER

I like to refer to my social circle as "boutique." My friends are all unique and high-quality and serve good food. But more than that, they teach me things about the world and myself that I couldn't learn anywhere else.

—DAN LEVY

It is nice to think how one can be recklessly lost in a daisy!

–ANNE MORROW LINDBERGH

One of the simplest
paths to deep change is
for the less powerful
to speak as much as they
listen and for the more
powerful to listen as
much as they speak.

–GLORIA STEINEM

Change will not come if we wait for some other person or some other time. We are the ones we've been waiting for. We are the change that we seek.

—BARACK OBAMA

Doing anything less than
something amazing is
squandering this whole
reason that you're here.

–BRANDON STANTON

There are years that
ask questions and
years that answer.

−ZORA NEALE HURSTON

✦ ✦ ✦

Friendship is the habitual
inclination to promote
the good in one another.

−EUSTACE BUDGELL

Think about winning the day ... If you are worried about the mountain in the distance, you might trip over the molehill right in front of you.

—*DREW BREES*

People always ask me, "You have so much confidence. Where did that come from?" It came from me. One day I decided that I was beautiful, and so I carried out my life as if I was a beautiful girl.

—*GABOUREY SIDIBE*

In order to be a realist you must believe in miracles.

—DAVID BEN-GURION

Home lies in the things
you carry with you
everywhere and not in the
ones that tie you down.

–PICO IYER

When there is danger, a good leader takes the front line; but when there is celebration, a good leader stays in the back of the room.

—*NELSON MANDELA*

When you lead with your nice foot forward, you will win, every time. It might not be today, it might not be tomorrow, but it comes back to you when you need it. We live in an age of instant gratification, of immediate likes, and it is uncomfortable to have to wait to see the dividends of your kindness. But I promise you it will appear exactly when you need it.

—KRISTEN BELL

I not only use all the brains that I have but all that I can borrow.

—*WOODROW WILSON*

✦ ✦ ✦

The problem with beauty is that it's like being born rich and getting poorer.

—*JOAN COLLINS*

Grief can change your outlook.
You don't ever forget the shock, the sadness, and the pain. But I do not believe that grief changes who you are. Grief, if you let it, will reveal who you are. It can reveal depths that you did not know you had. The startling weight of grief can burst any bubble of complacency in how you live your life, and help you to live up to the values you espouse.

—PRINCE WILLIAM, DUKE OF CAMBRIDGE

Everyone you will ever meet knows something you don't.

—BILL NYE

There are no hopeless situations; there are only people who have grown hopeless about them.

–*CLARE BOOTH LUCE*

✦ ✦ ✦

What I regret most in my life are failures of kindness.

–*GEORGE SAUNDERS*

I enjoy and am enjoying the good things that come along with [aging] ... Nobody can buy experience. Nobody can buy wisdom. Nobody can buy a shared history with others that you get by being relevant and engaged year upon year upon year.

—ROB LOWE

My generation was raised being able to flip channels if we got bored, and we read the last page of the book when we got impatient. We want to be caught off guard, delighted, left in awe.

—TAYLOR SWIFT

My mother always used
to say, "The older you get,
the better you get. Unless
you're a banana."

–BETTY WHITE

Thankfully, perseverance is a great substitute for talent.

–STEVE MARTIN

Those who don't know
how to weep with their
whole heart don't know
how to laugh either.

–GOLDA MEIR

I am not an optimist, because I am not sure that everything ends well. Nor am I a pessimist, because I am not sure that everything ends badly. I just carry hope in my heart. Hope is a feeling that life and work have a meaning. You either have it or you don't, regardless of the state of the world that surrounds you.

—VÁCLAV HAVEL

Excellence is not a singular act; it's a habit. You are what you repeatedly do.

–SHAQUILLE O'NEAL

Every child is an artist. The
problem is how to remain
an artist once we grow up.

–PABLO PICASSO

✦ ✦ ✦

A smile is truly the
best thing you can
put on your face.

–CHRISTIE BRINKLEY

Don't be scared if you don't do things in the right order ...
I didn't think I'd have dessert before breakfast today, but hey, it turned out that way and I wouldn't change a thing.

—MINDY KALING

Not everything is rational and not everything can be explained. If you don't allow some room for something poetic, for something magic, for something surprising, without the need to explain it away, you do a great disservice to your heart.

—*MARC MARON*

A peacock that rests on his feathers is just another turkey.

–DOLLY PARTON

There is a crack in
everything; that is how
the light gets in.

–LEONARD COHEN

✦ ✦ ✦

Never trust someone who
can't eat a meal alone at
their own kitchen table.

–ELLEN BARKIN

Families are like pieces of art– you can make them from almost anything, any kind of material. Sometimes they look like you and sometimes they don't. Sometimes they come from your DNA and sometimes they don't. The only ingredient you need to make a family is unconditional love.

—*MITCH ALBOM*

**If you don't listen eagerly
to the little stuff when [your
children] are little,** they won't
tell you the big stuff when they
are big, because to them, all of
it has always been big stuff.

—*CATHERINE M. WALLACE*

The most likely
moment for something
incredible to happen
to me was the moment
I was most certain
nothing ever would.

–JANE PAULEY

Be happy in your body ... It's the only one
you've got, so you might as well like it.
—KEIRA KNIGHTLEY

✦

You do your best work if you
do a job that makes you happy.
—BOB ROSS

✦

The reason people find it so hard to be happy is that
they always see the past better than it was, the present
worse than it is, and the future finer than it will be.
—MARCEL PAGNOL

Education and the warm heart–if you combine these two, then your education, your knowledge, will be constructive. You are yourself then becoming a happy person.
–THE DALAI LAMA

✦

I might not be famous one day. But I'd still be happy.
–SALMA HAYEK

✦

Mellow doesn't always make for a good story, but it makes for a good life.
–ANNE HATHAWAY

What an odd thing tourism is.
You fly off to a strange land, eagerly
abandoning all the comforts of
home, and then expend vast
quantities of time and money in a
largely futile attempt to recapture
the comforts that you wouldn't
have lost if you hadn't
left home in the first place.

—*BILL BRYSON*

The most important thing
a father can do for his
children is love their mother.

—*THE REV. THEODORE HESBURGH*

✦ ✦ ✦

Advice is what we ask for
when we already know the
answer but wish we didn't.

—*ERICA JONG*

I have been in love
many times, but I know
now that being in love
does not always mean you
know how to love.

–DIANE VON FURSTENBERG

Love, overflowing with small gestures of mutual care, is also civic and political, and it makes itself felt in every action that seeks to build a better world.

—*POPE FRANCIS*

One trouble with trouble is that it usually starts out like fun.

—ANN LANDERS

Treat a person as he is, and he will remain as he is. Treat him as he could be, and he will become what he should be.

–JIMMY JOHNSON

If there is one door in the castle you have been told not to go through, you must. Otherwise, you'll just be rearranging furniture in rooms you've already been in.

—ANNE LAMOTT

Everybody needs beauty
as well as bread, places to
play in and pray in, where
nature may heal and give
strength to body and soul.

–JOHN MUIR

Enthusiasm is everything.
It must be taut and vibrating
like a guitar string.

–*PELÉ*

✦ ✦ ✦

Most men pursue pleasure
with such breathless haste
that they hurry past it.

–*SØREN KIERKEGAARD*

My grandmother always used to say, "Summer friends will melt away like summer snows, but winter friends are friends forever."

—*GEORGE R. R. MARTIN*

I want to make music that helps.
'Cause that's the way I help.
I'm not a doctor. I'm not a lawyer.
I don't work in government.
I make music.

—LIZZO

I never learned anything while I was talking.

—LARRY KING

You don't get to choose
how you're going to die.
Or when. You can
only decide how you're
going to live. Now.

–JOAN BAEZ

I have this rule I live by:
Only do what you can do.
That means you're never looking
outside for what's popular;
you're always looking inside
for what's true.

—DELIA EPHRON

You don't have to be rich to live a rich life–and to me, taking time to prepare and enjoy food at a communal table with the ones you love is the best way to live richly.

—*RACHAEL RAY*

The cat could very well be
man's best friend but would
never stoop to admitting it.

–DOUG LARSON

✦ ✦ ✦

It takes less time to do a
thing right than to explain
why you did it wrong.

–HENRY WADSWORTH LONGFELLOW

We lift our gazes not to what stands between us but what stands before us. We close the divide because we know to put our future first, we must first put our differences aside. We lay down our arms so we can reach out our arms to one another. We seek harm to none and harmony for all.

—*AMANDA GORMAN*

The quieter you become, the more you can hear.

—RAM DASS

Not being funny
doesn't make you a bad
person. Not having a
sense of humor does.

✦ ✦ ✦

You can't build a reputation
on what you are going to do.

You don't just luck into things as much as you'd like to think you do. You build step by step, whether it's friendships or opportunities.

—*BARBARA BUSH*

The most remarkable thing about my mother is that for 30 years she served the family nothing but leftovers. The original meal has never been found.

—CALVIN TRILLIN

If you only read the
books that everyone else
is reading, you can
only think what everyone
else is thinking.

–HARUKI MURAKAMI

Great leaders are almost always great simplifiers.

—GEN. COLIN POWELL

It's a wonderful metaphor, catching a wave, for how you can look at other challenges in your life.

–JEFF BRIDGES

The unfortunate, truly exciting thing about your life is that there is no core curriculum ... So don't worry about your grade or the results or success. Success is defined in myriad ways, and you will find it, and people will no longer be grading you.

—*JON STEWART*

To be interested in
the changing seasons ...
is a happier state than
to be hopelessly
in love with spring.

–GEORGE SANTAYANA

Laughter brings the swelling down on our national psyche.

–STEPHEN COLBERT

✦ ✦ ✦

Success is a ladder that cannot be climbed with your hands in your pockets.

–AMERICAN PROVERB

No matter where you are in the world, somebody will be worse off than you. And if you think like that, you will always have the mindset to give back.

—*PRIYANKA CHOPRA*

Every single person I know (without exception) has had moments where they feel like they don't know which way is up. But I think part of the work we as humans are here to do is to learn to understand and have compassion for what is uncomfortable. Sadness and fear are a part of life (ask Pixar), and we can't pretend they don't exist. In fact, they enrich our lives.

—SARA BAREILLES

He who lives without discipline dies without honor.

–ICELANDIC PROVERB

An eye for an eye only
leads to more blindness.

–MARGARET ATWOOD

✦ ✦ ✦

I never panic when I
get lost. I just change
where it is I want to go.

–RITA RUDNER

Good leadership requires you to surround yourself with people of diverse perspectives who can disagree with you without fear of retaliation.

—*DORIS KEARNS GOODWIN*

We are all ordinary. We are all boring. We are all spectacular. We are all shy. We are all bold. We are all heroes. We are all helpless. It just depends on the day.

—*BRAD MELTZER*

A pessimist sees the
difficulty in every
opportunity; an optimist
sees the opportunity in
every difficulty.

–*WINSTON CHURCHILL*

You know what the greatest remedy on earth is today? ... It's not a pill. It's not a shot. It's a hug.

—BRUCE DERN

◆

All that is really worth the doing is what we do for others.

—LEWIS CARROLL

◆

Two important things are to have a genuine interest in people and to be kind to them. Kindness, I've discovered, is everything in life.

—ISAAC BASHEVIS SINGER

I've learned that people will forget what you said, people will forget what you did, but people will never forget how you made them feel.

—MAYA ANGELOU

✦

You never go wrong when you take the high road—it's less crowded up there.

—GAYLE KING

✦

Be kind to everyone because it costs you nothing and it takes you far.

—RACHEL BROSNAHAN

Plant seeds every single day that you know who you are, you know what you're about, and you know what goals you've set for yourself.

—STEPHEN CURRY

Smiling is definitely
one of my best
beauty remedies.

–RASHIDA JONES

✦ ✦ ✦

One child, one teacher,
one book, and one pen
can change the world.

–MALALA YOUSAFZAI

You have to create the
quiet to be able to
listen to the very faint
voice of your intuition.

–JON FAVREAU

It really is the greatest privilege given by one human being to another—to care for them at their most vulnerable time, to restore them to health when their bodies have betrayed them. They may barely know you, but at that moment, you're the most important person in their lives.

—DR. SANJAY GUPTA

The bird a nest, the spider a web, man friendship.

—WILLIAM BLAKE

Always bear in mind that your own resolution to succeed is more important than any one thing.

–ABRAHAM LINCOLN

We do not have to become heroes overnight. Just a step at a time, meeting each thing that comes up ... discovering we have the strength to stare it down.

—ELEANOR ROOSEVELT

A real friend is someone who takes a winter vacation on a sun-drenched beach and doesn't send a card.

–*FARMERS' ALMANAC*

This is a good sign, having a broken heart. It means we have tried for something.

–ELIZABETH GILBERT

✦ ✦ ✦

My father used to say, "If you want to be different, do something different."

–WYNTON MARSALIS

There's no drum roll or trumpet that goes off when you make the biggest decisions in your life. Sometimes you don't even know that you've made 'em.

—BEYONCÉ

You have those moments where you reflect. Wherever you're at–driving the car, in the plane, wherever–and you say, "No matter what I'm going through in life at the moment, from where I came from to where I am now, you know what? Life ain't bad."

—DWYANE WADE

It ain't what people call you. It's what you answer to.

–TYLER PERRY

That is what learning is.
You suddenly understand
something you've
understood all your life,
but in a new way.

–DORIS LESSING

Life is just a big extended improvisation. Embrace the ever-changing, ever-evolving world with the best rule I've ever found: Say "Yes, and..."

—*JANE LYNCH*

I was always told "Work hard when you're young so you can enjoy it when you're older." ... We should really be enjoying it all the way through. We shouldn't just say, "Well, let me be miserable now, and later ... then I'll be happy." You've got to learn to find the joy all the way.

—*MICHAEL STRAHAN*

Don't spend any time
whatsoever thinking about
what might have been.

–ALEX TREBEK

✦ ✦ ✦

Tension is who you think
you should be. Relaxation
is who you are.

–CHINESE PROVERB

Rare is the person who prefers the beauty found in the layers, the strata that develop over years of persevering through life and all its complications. Why don't we feel the urge to kiss the stretch marks that formed over the bellies that held our babies? The smile lines. Or the scars that tell part of our story: This happened to me.

—MOLLY RINGWALD

True giving happens when we give from our hearts.

—MUHAMMAD ALI

I do not think we have
a "right" to happiness.
If happiness happens,
say thanks.

–MARLENE DIETRICH

✦ ✦ ✦

Do or do not.

There is no try.

–YODA

Forgiving and being forgiven are two names for the same thing. The important thing is that a discord has been resolved.

—*C.S. LEWIS*

I don't believe in the generation gap. I believe in regeneration gaps. Each day you regenerate– or else you're not living.

—*DUKE ELLINGTON*

When I show my
daughter she can be
anything she wants to be,
she wonders why I ever
thought she couldn't.

–CANDACE PARKER

Don't aspire to make a living. Aspire to make a difference.

—DENZEL WASHINGTON

Even when I'm playing
someone named
Fat Amy, I'm all about
confidence and attitude.

–REBEL WILSON

Acts of creation are ordinarily reserved for gods and poets, but humbler folk may circumvent this restriction if they know how. To plant a pine, for example, one need be neither god nor poet; one need only own a shovel.

—*ALDO LEOPOLD*

Celebrate what you've
accomplished, but raise
the bar a little higher
each time you succeed.

–MIA HAMM

The way to gain a good
reputation is to endeavor to
be what you desire to appear.

—*SOCRATES*

✦ ✦ ✦

Candor is a compliment;
it implies equality.
It's how true friends talk.

—*PEGGY NOONAN*

My Grandpa Max the junkman would say in Yiddish, "The wheel is always turning." What he meant was how to behave toward people. The person on the bottom of the wheel, you'd better be nice to because at some point you're going to be on the bottom.

—*MANDY PATINKIN*

Life is short and we never have enough time for gladdening the hearts of those who travel the way with us. Oh, be swift to love! Make haste to be kind.

—*HENRI-FRÉDÉRIC AMIEL*

Speak the truth, but leave immediately after.

—SLOVENIAN PROVERB

A gentleman will not insult
me, and no man not a
gentleman can insult me.

–FREDERICK DOUGLASS

✦ ✦ ✦

You cannot do a kindness
too soon, for you never know
how soon it will be too late.

–RALPH WALDO EMERSON

**To be hopeful in bad times is
not just foolishly romantic.**
It is based on the fact that human
history is a history not only of
competition and cruelty but also
of compassion, sacrifice, courage,
kindness. What we choose to
emphasize in this complex history
will determine our lives.

—HOWARD ZINN

**With a song you can't explain
exactly what happens or when
it's going to happen** or what
it's going to do to you or
somebody else. But somehow,
it's this beautiful conduit
that connects everybody
in a way nothing else can.

—*ALICIA KEYS*

On the whole, human beings want to be good, but not too good, and not quite all the time.

–GEORGE ORWELL

*A good friend is a connection to life—
a tie to the past, a road to the future, the key
to sanity in a totally insane world.*

—LOIS WYSE

✦

**Only your real friends will
tell you when your face is dirty.**

—SICILIAN PROVERB

✦

Lots of people want to ride with you in the limo,
but what you want is someone who will take the
bus with you when the limo breaks down.

—OPRAH WINFREY

If you don't have a crazy Facebook friend,
you are the crazy Facebook friend.

—JIMMY KIMMEL

✦

The proper office of a friend is to side with you
when you are in the wrong. Nearly everyone
will side with you when you are in the right.

—MARK TWAIN

✦

*We need old friends to help us grow old
and new friends to help us stay young.*

—LETTY COTTIN POGREBIN

You can't get hung up on age or beauty, because then you're always chasing after something you'll never get back.

—*TINA TURNER*

If you can't change your
fate, change your attitude.

–AMY TAN

✦ ✦ ✦

There's no *them*. This is
what everybody does:
make a distinction about
them. It's just us.

–KEN BURNS

Some of the greatest conflicts are not between two people but between one person and himself.

–GARTH BROOKS

Searching is half the fun: life is much more manageable when thought of as a scavenger hunt as opposed to a surprise party.

—JIMMY BUFFETT

Giving never happens by accident. It's always intentional.

—AMY GRANT

You only have to do
a very few things right
in your life, so long
as you don't do too
many things wrong.

–WARREN BUFFETT

Never doubt that a small group of thoughtful, committed citizens can change the world. Indeed, it is the only thing that ever has.

—*MARGARET MEAD*